CONTENDING WITH THE DARK
Jeffrey Schwartz

AGAINST THAT TIME
Ron Schreiber

Cover and design by Deidre Moderacki
Cover photographs by David Socia and Deidre Moderacki

Thanks to the editors of the following publications, in which versions of
the poems from *Contending with the Dark* first appeared: *Aspect, Butt,
Dark Horse, Greenfield Review, Hanging Loose, Stone Soup,* and *Zeugma.*
The epigraph to "Lamia" is from "Rain" by John Ashbery. "Notes on
the Practice of Divination" is from *The Pictorial Key to the Tarot* by
Arthur Edward Waite, copyright © 1959 by University Books (Lyle
Stuart, Inc., Seacaucus, N.J.), by permission of the publisher.

Thanks for valuable assistance to Ed Hogan, Jeffrey Katz,
Mary Rothenbuehler, Tom Anderson, and CCI. (JS)

Thanks to the editors of the following publications in which versions of
the poems from *Against That Time* first appeared: *Aspect, Bachy, Dark
Horse, The Falcon, Fag Rag, Gay Sunshine, Hand Book, Lake Superior
Review, Man Root, Mati, Mouth of the Dragon, North American Review,
Painted Bride Quarterly, Phoebe, Pyramid, Silver (Seraphim II), Some,
Small Moon, Wind,* and *Windless Orchard.* "an hour ago you called"
appears in Allen De Loach's anthology *A Decade and Then Some,*
Buffalo: Intrepid Press, 1976. "the daimon is always other" is an
expression used by R.D. Laing. "Against that time (if ever that time
come)" is the first line of Shakespeare's forty-ninth sonnet.

The publication of this book was supported in part by a grant from the
National Endowment for the Arts, Washington, D.C., and assisted by the
Massachusetts Council on the Arts and Humanities.

ALICE JAMES BOOKS
138 Mt. Auburn Street
Cambridge, Massachusetts 02138

CONTENTS

Contending with the Dark

Against That Time

i. all the little things are fine

ii. picnicking in Sitka

CONTENDING WITH THE DARK

for Edith Wetsel
(1952-1975)

MODELING BLINDFOLD

You are having a head
made of your final expression.
The sculptor, your employer,
has tied a scarf around your eyes
and said don't move.

You sense her face orbiting
and closing in on yours.
She wants an instant accumulation
of years, all the loves
and losses in one look.

Cold damp fingers
transfer hills and caverns
to your clay head.

Without looking you can't tell
how soon you will be finished.
You have time, maybe too much,
to think about the past,
but there are distractions.

The sculptor's touch
and her breath
and her cool insistence that death
is what makes you concentrate
excite and distress you
until your arms begin to wander.

You are near calling it off,
telling her this is too much to ask,
when something
a finger? a bullet? her lips?
kisses your forehead.

THE OLD CEMETERY

Trees block my way to the grave
but I get there
                I bring a dog
who disappears behind the old stones
fog horns. no moon
stars are behind clouds
windswept. trees
bend. and climb

I do a dance feeling for
                         stretching
for the horizontal the earth
I can't penetrate
                the earth
cold
you already are part of

It's under me

under treescarves
and banners
              I go down
to kiss
and smear the dirt
on my face
              to become you
to know you in

your rock
your sleep
your death

LYING IN THE ROAD

If each star was a familiar place
I wouldn't have to worry
about headlights
                    A screen slams
and the cows moo down the road
Your dirt driveway
leads to a dark house of sleepers
        The hay is still
where the old man mowed it today

I never saw so many stars

One lit for each of us
When I find mine
I can relax

That one arcs out of sight
like your friend
        who died today at 23
Cancer burned in her
till the perforations overlapped
                    and she fell through

Fire Shooting Electrocution Drowning Disease
Explosion or just Painless fading: parables
your grandmother told this week
to make me tough

She steered me past 70 years
of places I'll never see
but I nodded like the old farmer

He wants it all tonight

                    We lie awake together
me on this tar and the farmer
next to his barren wife
both of us exposed to the facts
        but resisting
                    stubborn
listening for cars

FACES OF EGYPT

Old Egypt, have I known you too long?
Your lips read like the morning paper.
Last night I sat up and jerked
out of a dream I have
about crossing the desert to you.

It was 2 am (later
someone said I screamed, *Egypt, thank God!*).
The fan blades slowed, distinct,
and there was sand in the sheets.

At breakfast I checked.
You were still there,
the coffee-ringed accomplice
I had grown to expect,
changed into the travel ad
I prayed to after work.

Set unreachable goals,
selling used cars taught me.
Dreaming, I would crawl the desert
in a Plymouth
hauling the sun to a neon horizon.

I could have imagined myself awake,
but I was mad for your touch.
Egypt, how should I act with you in the room?
You showed up this morning like Gregor Samsa
turned suddenly real
and who can I tell? who will believe?

HOMES GONE

I go to movies to remember
growing up in Ohio with only mysteries
that could be solved, expected endings.

That was the life. If I came in on time
I got fed and no one asked who I was
or what I was going to be.

Changing cities so fast, I forget
where I've spent the most time. Ohio
a family, the years that passed flat as film

resurface and fade out of reach.
I have to watch other people
to keep things straight, and sometimes

at dusk before the shades are pulled,
I'll feel it threatening from next door,
some family calling me into the warm light.

FLORIDA (LAND OF FLOWERS)

In the oldest settled state
where my grandparents have gone,
the palm leaves are falling off.
60 is too cold to sleep
without bringing kerosene stoves
in from the shed. This year
they have lived longer
than any migrants on the block—
fellow northerners or the Cubans,
whom they resent. Every time
I fly down at Christmas
I take the same walk past the same houses
decorated with lights and winter scenes
indifferent to the temperature.
I look in the porches and listen
to songs sung in Spanish, the language
spoken 450 years ago
by Juan Ponce de Leon, the first
to want everything in Florida
to stay the same. Car metal that rots
from the salt air and the palm trees
choked with disease will be gone
and be replaced. Those who want to survive
like natives learn to move slowly
and be suspicious of change.

UP ON MT. ARCHER

A deer hangs in the barn
between a Datsun 510 wagon
and a Sears snowblower.
While the raw meat hardens
in the cold, darker and darker
over the old newspapers,
firelight fills half
of the U-shaped house.
On one side the young couple pass
cocktails to their city guests
and on the other, digital clocks click
in the husband's office in the dark.

Years ago there were so many deer
that the father could walk
like a photographer into a herd,
pose them, step back, and shoot.
The son is the first to need
to be shrewd. For days
he goes out in camouflage
trailing the warm turds
and the wet leaves bent
into the print of a cleft hoof.
No one before him ever had to pay
for food or make the distinction
between home life and work.

On a few drinks the guests
are feeling connected to the land,
to the self-sufficiency of their host
chopping wood and hunting
on Mt. Archer. After dinner
he will lead them out
to see the carcass hanging
skinned and hollowed in the barn,
its deer-like features buried
or scattered over ground used
since Uncas or before.

THE HAWK

1.

The hawk looks down
at its short belly feathers
white as inside apples
each dabbed with the copper
of winter fields.
Its great wings, too heavy to lift,
are bathed in a river breeze
that for January is warm.

The hawk is somewhere
no one has looked.

2.

Today as it was flying over the old marsh
known to strengthen around men's boots and throats,
it heard the familiar song of the hunters,
felt its eyes scorch with memories,
and fell here beside the stone wall.

3.

Under my fingers your heart softens
in a nest of bones—
the only way I could have known you.

The short feathers that fall into my hand
like bright coins are memories
you give me to protect.

ON A MOUNTAIN AT NIGHT

We sat in two chairs
abandoned in a field
not that we needed them
but by then we had learned
to make use of obstacles
& there was no danger of cars
or other people & the brandy
kept our blood warm.

Unburdened of any reason
to be elsewhere we noticed
for the first time
the brilliance of the sky
& as the alcohol burned
& your lips turned apricot
the wooden arms that first
attracted us fell away.

NOTE LEFT AFTER BEING RECOGNIZED IN A CROWDED CAFE

Remember when I found you staggering in Harvard Square
and you told me about the proposal you had been working on
for over a year that couldn't get funded and how it was
crippling you and you had to let go but you couldn't because
you had invested so much energy and it was going to save the world
and finally it had driven you to drinking up your paychecks
and you had to move into a place with five couples who wanted to eat
dinner at the same time, share every responsibility, and talk
about sexual frustration?

And remember how I listened to you that night and filled you
with hope that the proposal could work if only it had a
fresh point of view and someone who would take it around again
because it was sure to catch on? It was all a matter of priorities
I said as though it were the first time and that the proposal
would save the culture and wipe out deviance because finally, finally
there would be a standard of laws that everyone would accept.
And then remember when I borrowed the proposal and said
I would be the one to spread the word and continue your work?

Well, I lied.

SOMETIMES, BECAUSE IT WAS ENDING

Sometimes, because it was ending,
our fingers went
wild; our eyes
told everything.

Other times, words,
too clumsy
with purpose
slowed us down.

I was no soldier
used to occasional love,
prepared never
to be surprised.

When we walked
hand in hand
through your city
we were reckless with time

as if we weren't concerned
with memories, as if
we would never need
to remember.

THE AIR AT DUSK

Hershey H., why do I think of you now
mourning my love on Beacon Street
with the windows open?
Why do you and your annoying red hair
reappear suddenly fourteen years
and a dozen addresses later?
I can remember beating you up
on the sewer lid in my driveway,
so close we could have slow-danced,
and splitting your tight wet lips
till they bled like cherries.
I remember taking the clothes off
of your sister's paper dolls,
molesting your mother's tomato plants,
and the smell of your garage
where the gray dog lived, the Weimaraner,
with a dick for a tail.
How did this first spring air
remind me of you?

Because it is spring, Hersh,
and because this is the air
we played in until dark and because
the past is out of control.
When my love died,
the winter fooled me into thinking
there were no different times,
and now the warm weather returns
the months when I knew her
on Marlborough Street, a block away.
All the memories I could summon or avoid
don't pierce deep as these
that arrive by themselves, triggered
by some recurrent detail that shocks, quick,
and might have slipped away unnamed.

SPARKS FROM HEAVEN

There was going to be a revelation
(I could tell by his look)

a boy deceived by the purity
of an encircled star came first
followed by:
a woman in bed with her eyes covered,
ten swords piercing the flesh of the same man,
two lovers exchanging cups,
a bent woman. . .

see *Notes on the Practice of Divination:*

1. Before beginning the operation, formulate
   your question definitely, and repeat it aloud.
2. Make your mind as blank as possible while
   shuffling the cards.
3. Put out of the mind personal bias and preconceived
   ideas as far as possible, or your judgement will be
   tinctured thereby.
4. On this account it is more easy to divine correctly
   for a stranger than for yourself or a friend.

It was still new to him. . .
a bent woman in a shawl and wool socks,
a pair of dogs crazy from the scorpion bite of the moon,
a man carrying a bundle of wands taller than he

He arranged those pictures
in the shape of a cross

The pictures are doors
opening into unexpected chambers
or a turn in the open road
with a wide prospect beyond

Between reading the cards he told me:

"Once the pictures come alive

I see the man & woman & dog parts
of myself—you have to get close enough
to have something inside you sparked off

It's a matter of allowing
my associations to mingle

then to follow them,
their patterns

I live the chronology of the cards
changed with each step

—what's important is the final experience
which gives the parts another meaning"

These he placed one above the other
along the right-hand side:

a man upside down with one knee bent
and his head on a golden pillow,
a king entering New York City with four coins,
a boy in fear of poles that grow leaves,
a nude pouring out all the pots

The mere numerical powers
and names of the cards
are insufficient by themselves

I believed the pictures,
from the Page of Pentacles to the Star,
not because it made my life sensible

but because he could see
how others had seen them before and how

"by concentrating on the cards
we find something
in their magical order

that they can make true"

NOTHING BUT OMENS

Already the Cumberland Farms burned down
an old lover returned
a new one vanished
the weather jumped to extremes
and tonight
a Cadillac ricocheted a Dodge
off my parked car

There are signs
the way changes come all at once
Nothing is accidental

Events like death
that could have been predicted
make sense afterward
summing up the coincidences
the signs that pass too quickly
into the dark

Last week I moved here
and tomorrow I start a new job
It all fits

the fire and the rain
and the passing of love

MYSTIC ROOMS

She was raised by the sea,
extracted from a salty flame
with potter's hands. They
like things centered but
not straight. Not smooth,
not light as her cat.

She lived in the cold
rooms of cities working
to know them as a kid learns
the sound of her name.
Once fire came. It put
her trunk on the street.

It killed her cat.
She moves on. The branches
crack under cold rain.
Brown bricks hide scenes of
people meeting for the first time.
Smokestacks pump cantabile

for the dancers outside.
There are four ways to read
this poem: from the street,
in the fire, singing, or out
of her hands shaping—
raising the walls of wet clay.

THE FLAMING CAR

How long did I drive
before catching fire?
How long down the avenue
with your name before
smoke crowded me out?

An unmarked wedding passed
blowing horns and people
on the sidewalk pointed
frantic, out of control.

When I pulled to the curb
and stepped out, firemen
rushed screaming in.

I watched them let loose
hosing the engine and seats
hacking at smoke on
the dashboard, the glass.

Was it love of duty
or destruction made them grin
as they snuffed out the last breath?
I thought I recognized you
among the volunteers.
They saved me and were gone.

BIOGRAPHY

for Henry Strater

You came as Father Time
in emperor's gown and patriotic socks,
a plunger for his scythe.
In the kitchen sipping a beer
you said you painted:
houses I thought
or a Provincetown amateur
soaking the summer rich.

What convinced me was
Charles Demuth and Marsden Hartley.
WCW I could relate to
and your interview on the Today Show.
Still I didn't act like you were famous.
Anyone could have driven ambulances
with Dos Passos and Hem.

Dizzying, you steered yourself
away from the sink.
Words don't do like the canvasses
you drew naked girls behind.
You had to grow old to be recognized.
You never wanted to blow off your head.

DOWNSTAIRS FROM THE MAN WITH THE KNACK

Ladies line up on the stairs
outside his room all wearing
the same sweater dresses
and heavy chain medallions.
Every hour one leaves
past my door and disappears.

In Liverpool there's a girl
who paints rooms with a radio
turned up, scat singing
like Annie Ross to the old jazz.
She comes over unannounced
and has to muscle through the crowd.

We make love with them outside
listening to us
like to a documentary warm-up
and I wonder
if he ever gets hurt
or has to worry about raising

a family. I'm like him
making no promises
pretending this girl is unique.
When she sings and I like it
I'm lucky
and sometimes she spends the night.

THE LANDLADY'S SCARS

the landlady has a different wig
in the attic for every man
that has popped her the question
they come to the door
& knock & knock until
I have to let them in
& they breeze past me grinning
bloodhounds every one of them
but suckers for a disguise

after the soap operas
& they leave
& it's safe to slip out
in her own hair & an old robe
she leans on the railing
a dark Harlow
gracefully & smokes

she'll go up to the attic
to impersonate her wild affairs
or come over to my place
& reminisce about the dumb ones
the close calls or the scars
for which no man lives long enough
to be forgiven

LAMIA

The day of the week will not save you.

Someone is in the backyard hanging herself
or in your room spreading her legs

She is the one we warned you about
who waits for you after school
or calls on the phone & doesn't talk

You shut your eyes
& she is still there

What do you do now when someone acts
like she is in your dream

when the lights go on
& you are not alone

When you used to have nightmares
we would say:
breathe out the window

If something went wrong:
there'll be another day

ALL YOUR MEN

I lit a sand candle.
Under the rabbit skin
shawl your guts showed.
My smooth skin
made you nervous.

You took your toy saw
down from my chin
to my asshole
spooned the insides
and dried them like shells
on your bed.

You fingered my past—
my places
my women my fears and
tasted them.
You gave me yours,
made me all your men
then squint
that my voice
familiar looses time.

THE SCULPTOR'S BEDROOM

postcards of the dead
strapped standing to a wall
in Mexico their mouths
forever open
                a museum
to the final contractions of life

It took away the holiness
I lived across from a slaughterhouse
where they butchered pigs. Pigs
cried in the night. Bullfighters
invoked God there
by turning their backs
Believers in fate. People
whose faces I wanted to touch

two skulls from Mexico
on the sill one a child's
the other cracked in thirds
from the impact of a bullet
entering behind the right ear

to hold onto the physical beyond life. . .

I used to paint. Stay awake for 3 days
painting, painting in a trance but the colors
were too emotional. Made me crazy
I had to stop

her heads
       bronze
       clay
       plaster
        cement
and her animals crafted
to look like the original

in bed
in the self-portrait over the bed
first her forehead shows broad
as the hairless stone skulls
on the sill
and then her eyes
more fearful than the ones
her thumbs pressed
peer from the sheets
                her eyes

a petrified rat in childbirth
I found in a drawer in New Hampshire

behind the hair
behind the clay masks
into the cold

hold no fear of death

CONTENDING WITH THE DARK

The trees clap their bony wrists in the air calling back
their shadows growing away from them, bending downhill.
It is happening again. At the end of a day
a man appears at a certain cabin. He kicks loose
the iron hatch of the stove and stirs dormant embers
into night-long jewels of heat. *Beware, beware*
the wind howls, freezing the short rain on the snow
and in the joints of the trees. A mouse twitches,
a little death, each time the wind seethes through the walls.
If they're warm, the mice are invisible. They don't care
that the man's family has a history of fire
or that there are cities in him that never healed.
He hears the trees over him rubbing like wooden spoons
and sleeps wrapped in the shadows of their long arms.

TREE DREAM

An old man three times my age
was splitting wood with arms
wider than his sleeves.
Delicately he started a wedge
into either end of the one-foot logs
letting loose a geyser of sap
separating fibers that kept cracking
between blows. The wet wood wanted
to stick together like skin.

He pried apart one and faced me
and I took the wood in my hands
stroking the purple core and the meat
and learned the taste and hugged it
that it would know warmth before fire
and I would not put it down
and I could not find any tree in it
though it had been one once
and now lay sprawled bloodless
in pieces over the ground.

HUNGERING

after Hamsun

1.

In the last photo of the Norwegian hotel
you can make out the backs
of the landlady and a longshoreman
with a sailor's chest on his shoulder.
She has a crucifix on her arm,
a butterfly on her breast,
a rose inside her thigh.
They were about to enter my room
overlooking the little yards
behind Vognmands Street.

2.

I sell the newspaper pictures
of savage accidents or views of Christiania.
They go for ten kroner each,
but it doesn't pay the rent.
Yesterday the landlady kicked me downstairs
to live with her family
in a hallway off the kitchen.

3.

In the safe of the Food & Lodging for Travelers
are photos of the landlady making love
across the room from her paralyzed father.
There are photos of her four kids
waving blurry feathers in the old man's ears.
There are photos of the landlady
introducing her husband to the new guests.
There are self-portraits of me with the landlady.

4.

To keep away hunger:
I could pawn my camera.
I could demand food for her "souvenirs."
I could stop taking pictures
and go to work in a grocery.
I could sign onto the next ship to Cadiz.

5.

At dawn faces in the hallway materialize
like images in a darkroom,
or a feast before a beggar.
Today if I have to
I will pawn my leather shoes
for a package of film.

BUNDLING

> The sofa in summer is more dangerous
> than the bed in winter.
>> –Samuel Peters, 1781

Remember the night you couldn't
get home and my parents
fastened their ears to the walls?
They set you up on the convertible
in the den and I stayed
till the channels sang "America."
We moved with the furnace,
whenever the burner lit.
Clothes kept us apart.
Buttonholes like swollen jambs.
Zippers only a field marshal could command.
Oh how we schemed that night.
If only we had deserved the eyes
they gave us at breakfast.

"IT'LL NEVER HAPPEN AGAIN"

The assurance
hangs in the air
over my rolling
sleeping body.

What will never happen?
You'll never leave,
we'll never argue,
you'll never come back?

For a second I remembered
you packed
& already departed.
This time for good.

Something will not happen
hardly matters
if what is missing
is you.

THE FIRST ANNIVERSARY

The way the leaves are released
from the four big maples
where there used to be five
in front of your neighbors' stone fence

reminds me of you dancing
in your father's story about the year
you turned into a woman.

And the subdued colors along the Connecticut
were the same the day he and I
sailed up to Hamburg Cove

only then I didn't know the friends
who when the *Edith West* passed
looked down with the shame of survivors.

And the cherry vines knotted over the bridge
in the old farm graveyard
where you wanted to be married

grip tight as the pallbearers' drive
here to where we set you down.

THE SECOND ANNIVERSARY

Yesterday at Tom's wedding
I watched the fall colors at their peak
melt into mist and night sky.

It is still raining. "The weather
never affected me as much as this."
"When the end of the world comes

will we be together?" Two years ago
today I got caught in the rain
without a hat or an umbrella

but like you, for once, I didn't care.
I was soaked on the bus with everyone
packed in, shivering

realizing out loud we're
all gonna die. We only could see
ourselves in the steamed windows.

A month ago Martha was married
a few miles from where you grew up.
Now she will feel no rain.

Now she will feel no cold.
I have learned not to expect
anything to keep its shape.

Even you grow less discernible.
"Now you are one body. Go. Enter
into the days of your togetherness."

LOVE POEM

Accumulating your things,
I become you.
I put on your habits, your clothes.
I write at your desk, read your letters.
I start talking like you,
saying *get it together*
or *you're too blasé.*
I call the cat with your old names.
The room reverberates with you.

If you had only gone elsewhere,
say, home for good,
or back to Europe.
If you had gone on an extended vacation to Alaska
or to live with an old lover in Ohio.
I might have left everything,
turned over my life.
I could have been sustained
by the very fact of your existence.

This way we live together more permanently
than if you were here.
You settle into the room
and I ask myself,
is this the independence we craved;
what about balance?
There isn't any balance.
I carry you weightlessly
wherever I move.

PUTTING ON THE DREAM ROBE

Let's talk about everything we like to avoid
everything we don't understand
or so obvious we neglect
Everything that drives us

Let's do what we have to & know why
say the things there weren't words for
and lower deeper deep into our souls
Let this be an excavation

for what we have had in common
& what keeps us apart
Let's not remember to take pains
or mince words or make sense

Let's put on the dream robe
that we wear to shit & die in
And let's move in a frenzy of touch
unsettling everything

tonguing the dark secrets
the speleologist's curse
And let's have it all for once
be everything & let that be it

A Gainſt that time (if euer that time come)
  When I ſhall ſee thee frowne on my defeꞔs,
When as thy loue hath caſt his vtmoſt ſumme,
Cauld to that audite by aduiſ'd reſpeꞔs,
Againſt that time when thou ſhalt ſtrangely paſſe,
And ſcarcely greete me with that ſunne thine eye,
When loue cõnuerted from the thing it was
Shall reaſons finde of ſetled grauitie.
Againſt that time do I inſconce me here
Within the knowledge of mine owne deſart,
And this my hand,againſt my ſelfe vpreare,
To guard the lawfull reaſons on thy part,
    To leaue poore me,thou haſt the ſtrength of lawes,
    Since why to loue,I can alledge no cauſe.

i.   all the little things are fine

"the daimon is always other"

windshield covered with
snow churned up
by passing truck wheels:
a car skids.
a guardrail runs to meet it.

a daimon inhabits his body,
nourishes drag races & ice.
hands grip the wheel.
whose fingers?

the car is driven.
who drives the car?

coming down from Notre Dame

gargoyles at the top.
I watch a German boy,
talk to him, arrange
to meet next morning,
when I wait two hours,
then go about my business.
which is touring.
the rose window.

Russ & I alternate driving.
the one on the right
watches for good-looking
hitchhikers, but he always
says "that one" after the
driver's gone by. we
pick up a Belgian boy,
sophisticated & delectable.
we drop him off at Nîmes.
we keep our fantasies.

twice I fall in love:
with Mauro in Florence,
with Knud in Copenhagen.
I visit luxurious apartments
& back alleys. I visit
museums. I eat well.

returning to America is
as easy as falling in love.

Amsterdam Avenue &
Cathedral Parkway: the
rose window melts.

a family visit

going to never-never land:
Miami, Fort Lauderdale, Boca
Raton, where I never grow old.

to my mother I'm still a child
of 3, or 12, or 20, all my past
washed in the same machine,

rinsed & wrung together, hung
out to dry, undifferentiated.
to my father I'm a kaleidoscopic

slide show, sometimes attractive
& sometimes he doesn't like
to look at pictures.

visiting two people I used to
live with, I forget the old lines,
& the prompter stayed in Ohio

when they moved south. foot-
lights glare & blind, but we're not
acting in the same play anymore.

instructions

Wait one week
(until I've left for the summer).
Don't close the doors of the hot room I sleep in.
Don't shut the windows & leave me to sweat until
I wake up in the middle of the night.

Twice I was shot in the head.
My mother told me about it on the way to the hospital.
By the time the ambulance got there I had lost too much blood.
By the time I woke up I had died.

Open the windows.
Don't close the doors of the room I sleep in.
Wait one week.

inertia, 1971

last night you wondered if it might not be best
to take your days off on my work days   nothing seems to happen
when we're free together   I watch the seventh game of the Series
you read a novel that you've read before
when I come into the room you fall asleep

today you have a cold or maybe bronchitis   it's easy to blame you
when you're sick   or when you're healthy   all you want to do
is watch the soaps in the afternoon or go out to dinner
because cooking's such a drag

                                but I'm the same way only nervous
projects flash across my mind like comets burning out
till everything that shines becomes a number on a list
washing the kitchen floor & making love are 16 & 24
our bodies harden from exercises we do together every morning
but we don't know what to do with our bodies

                                & there's no blame
we're tired after work   we don't bring each other autumn daisies
we don't go out to see the leaves change color   or dull our senses
at the movies   you hear music all day when you work so you don't
play records any more   I seldom did

                                & there's no blame
lethargy sits in my head like a hippopotamus in mud   rolling over
when flies start to itch that iron skin   sometimes I sit
& listen to the clock

                        maybe tomorrow when winter comes
we'll think about the garden neither of us planted this fall
maybe we'll miss the leaves we didn't see
or maybe those cold winds will lash our faces
& we'll shield our eyes & suddenly become alert

but winter is a hard season this far north   can't there be a way now
for our signs to mix   earth & air   air & earth   or else to
rest together in the same bed

                        no blame the oracle says
I can't read what else it says about us   there are invisible
bulky walls in the house whenever one of us walks through
that can't be seen or touched   & since they form impenetrable space
between us   it's hard to know what colors we can paint them
or find the brush   & take it in our hands

stuffed ears

for the first time in a year
I'm sick again, again in winter.
my ears are stuffed.

I don't hear messages.
I don't need you here every night.
don't need you to love my friends.

I need you when I'm swimming
(I'm not a dolphin or a bass).
or when I try to fly
(I'm not a gull).

looking over my shoulder,
I try to see footsteps.
sometimes I need you

to open a window
when I can't see anything.
touch me now.

first day in Truro

our five rooms have been a small prison
where I don't remember what I dream at night
& little poems drip from a leaky faucet
--brown rust in porcelein   this morning I struggled
like Jacob & shreds of dream unwound
I stretched to greet the sun
planted herbs in sandy soil before I ate
--ocean air in my head & stomach--

late morning I spent with women at the laundromat
one other man   a big crewcut midwesterner
was there to help his wife
I washed musty towels & sheets
three machines three dry spins each
the afternoon I walked into the valley
below the house to pick up wood & ticks
I finished reading another woman's book
all I feel comfortable with after years
of learning what men have to teach:
how to reason   how to compete   how to control

again at night I dreamt   I walked
with my Russian brothers & made love with them
we talked of Williams & of Whitman
& I dug those blond faces open to America
the space of plains & tundra & Indian grasslands
the roar of polluted falls in Paterson
a bridge across the East River   across the Dnieper
the frozen soil of Siberia
the sandy soil of Cape Cod

St. Nicolaas Dag

i. past
it's far from the plains of Nebraska
to the Pacific coast. the Donner party
froze in the snows of Nevada mountains.
some survived. when food ran out
they ate each other. to live
meant to be a cannibal: a natural act,
an act of survival.

ii. present
you wear long dresses when I see you,
buy new clothes to wear to work.
manage a store of bright colors
& a household every day. go out
to bars & parties. sometimes you barely sleep.
you are so many persons
at night alone in bed I dream
of your prismatic changes.

iii. now
the distance from Back Bay to Somerville
is not so far. one river separates us.
according to the Farmers Almanac
it will be cold & wet all winter,
& bleak in Boston without you.
in March we can walk across the Charles.
in April we can swim.

the twelfth of June

1. This time you're leaving, not me. But I feel the motion, the first circle of a whirling vortex, not our move into a new house with Tom & Mary & Tim & Susan & four cats & the dog Sunny, but with you in a 747 going to London & *Amstel-re-dam en je eigen vader en Tini en Frans en al de kinderen.*

2. I'll stay here. I'll be here when you return.

3. We aren't lovers anymore. We've lost the webs we spun to catch each other.

4. We aren't spiders anymore. The webs are broken, & we've each lost six of our eight legs.

5. Your room is finished--the sink removed & the walls painted. Our cats recognize the room from your bed & the familiar furniture.

6. For a month you won't be in your room. Sometimes I'll be there -to get to know the cats again while you're gone--what I'd planned o do when I lived with you again for three weeks but could not do because that was not the way.

7. & I worked on the house with Mary & Tom & Tim, whom I pushed & prodded from deep wells of my anxiety & nervous energy. & that was not the way either.

8. The last two nights, sleeping in the haunted room where Susan will live, I dreamed & dreamed & refused to remember the dreams. But I know my dreams are haunted by ghosts of our past together & ghosts of my own past growing up with my parents surrounded by people who shuffle money & social standing & deal away their dreams.

9. This time you're leaving, & I'm staying home. This time the vortex is not a spiral of jet engines or car motors, but the motion is even swifter.

10. In Muiden there is a castle with a dry moat we've walked across together when we lived in Amsterdam & your parents lived in Purmerend & we all drove together in our three-cylinder Volkswagen to Steenwijk & Broek-in-Waterland.

11. Remember me to Tante Joh when you see her tomorrow in Edam. Remember me to Tini & to Frans & to your brothers & your sisters-in-law. Remember me to your father, for he is also the father who knows & loves me. Remember me to your mother when you dream of her, for she adopted me into your family.

12. Fly well; when you sleep *wel te rusten.* Rimpie & Mijnsje will miss you; I'll feed them twice a day. We will be here in the middle of August, when you return, spinning from Amsterdam & London, up & down the three floors of our new house, spinning in place, whirling in perpetual motion.

three trays of slides

i.

new slides of all the people
in the house: Brian holding Slago,
a monstrous dog. slides from
Plymouth: Tom walking in reeds,
smiling. Randy & Darrell together.
you haven't met Darrell. you don't
see Randy anymore. you haven't
seen these slides.

ii.

I first took
color pictures in Japan in 1956,
with a Petri camera I bought at
the PX & still use now. my hair
was peacetime army short. Bill
didn't have any hair & that didn't
bother me at all. I was
much younger then & I wasn't happy.

iii.

six years ago in Heath:
Larry offers you a joint; you hug him
while he holds a cigarette. Peggy's
laughing on a fall day by a waterfall.
you're holding a baby, laughing.
how easy it seemed then.
how carefree you look.

all the little things are fine

five days a week: out at nine   home by seven.
fabrics in bright colors envelope you as you work.
nearly every evening we eat together.
at night we sleep   & when we want to
& we're not too tired or too shy
we make love.

but the gap between my words & your silence feels like a canyon
–not one army engineers would dam for power & recreation,
more like the 100-foot gorge behind John's house in Trumansburg
without walls or fences. the water's swift there in spring
& summer. tourists drive up to look over the edge.
there's only one bridge across the falls;

                                        we cross it together.
we stand in the center & peer down into the wild stream.

February thaw

Monday. will we get a free subscription? Tom asks.
no *House & Gardens* till the name on our mailbox
pays his bills. but others arrive--send no money,
they advertise, & we get free books & begonias,
silver spoons & tiny wooden shoes.

Tuesday. a woman from *Mademoiselle*
visits our workshop. she plans to feature us
in an article about cooperative businesses. *Madame,*
one says in France to women over 24; *Mevrouw* in Holland.
does my mother in Florida still play bridge with the girls?

Sunday. four male editors read manuscripts.
a poet writes how she is fulfilled only as mother,
only as wife. I want to read her lines ironically,
but she means it, a lush catalogue of services & chores.

February thaw. we read books, prepare soil for begonias.
a freelance writer does what she can between cake
& cosmetics. one of the girls cuts the deck.
my mother bids four no-trump.
there was supposed to be a storm in Boston yesterday.
it never came.

around

a marionette, wooden &
painted in gay colors,
an intricate carving,
even the mouth opened
to laugh & sometimes speak.

sometimes he used to
shout at it when no one listened.
in August the strings broke
from overuse or age, or
something just wore out.

something that wears out
exhausts him when he tries
to make it go. or angers
him when he caresses it.
in October it broke in pieces.

it broke into pieces yesterday.
the right arm still stuffs
envelopes, the left hand types.
the penis pretends to have sex.
but the head piece is missing.

the head is missing.
even the mouth that used
to open to laugh or speak
has broken into pieces.
something wore out.

a distance from survival

*middle class fantasies oppress the
middle class & every class beneath it.*

eleven people downstairs
the tables set for dinner

I want to be the maid
clearing dirty dishes

drinking every leftover
swallow from wine glasses

scraping food from plates
for my own late stew.

there is heating oil enough
for every fifteenth room

tomorrow you'll be wrapped
warm in the streets

--while it rains in Boston
& Irish winos shiver on

stoops I long to sweep
one broom stroke at a time.

stage directions

--are you pissed off?
--no, but I'm tired of running out of time.

something frozen, waiting to thaw.
dreams keep me in bed another half-
hour, but I don't remember them.
only melting icicles, a committee
meeting, something somebody said
on the stairs, going down.

I start to gag on what I hear:
a woman writing from the deep
south, the chill of her new husband.
or dying: Tom's father in Florida
last week; Ferg in Scituate,

waiting for spring, the last season.
Michele in Washington, dying at 40,
my own age. another birthday party
this week & every candle on the cake
tells where we've been. no light

for where we're going. *calm &*
energy, I say at the store,
buying ginseng tablets. *the same*
as meditation, only American, you
just pop a pill. a man comments,
you ought to try living.

I've tried it, I tell him. *I'm*
still trying. Eliot lied about April,
but the soil is rocky & root-filled.
:exit quietly. close the door behind you.
turn out the lights.

something is happening

we bounce on trampolines,
send roots into the sky,
mislay plumblines, & we
don't want anybody to know.

ii.   picnicking in Sitka

people I like are not out to get me

       i.

they have a nice herb garden & they don't
like the weeds I plant there.

       ii.

houses create their inmates.
--thousands of walls but no windows.

       iii.

I brought a truck & a sick lover to Boston.
there's got be a slow train out.

living in the same place

you died last night
Jim & Lillian walked by in tears
then Serena   looks of horror
on their faces   then your Jim
a forced smile like the smile
of the black nurse who told me
Martin Luther King was shot
nearly hysterical   fighting back
his tears   "it's Linda; she's
dead" someone said
"I know" Jim said

you'd been playing together
running through a cave
hide-&-seek it must have been
there was a hole   a deep pit
& you disappeared   maybe you wanted
to plunge into that darkness
maybe you didn't   you died
last night   I felt the shock
when I awakened

                      now you're here
planning the day's activities
shopping   cooking breakfast
& I'm angry with you
there wasn't time to adjust
my head feels like a ping-pong ball
bounced by sandpaper paddles on a wood table
be one thing or the other
stay on your side of the net
keep out of my dreams

speculations

i.

a gay liberation meeting at the Red Book. that was the first time
I saw you, you said you were a poet. you seemed to be cruising &
no one cruised there, not that I saw. maybe you were cruising me,
& I could't understand that at all. I was not comfortable with you.
not then. not later, when six of us met every Sunday for a year.
the good gay poets, we called ourselves. but I began to like you.
I always listened to you because you talked a lot.

ii.

you studied piano for eight years
& stopped when you were ready
to play recitals, compete
for concert space. you are oldest
of three sons, who learned to cook
from your grandmother. like good cooks
you don't spare ingredients or pots.
you don't buy food & you don't clean up.
your meals are good to eat.

you went to Yale & dropped out.
joined a white auxiliary of the Panthers,
at ease in that third world,
calling yourself dark, as dark as they.
you know more facts & theories than
anyone, & you talk about them.

& never man or man enough.
a faggot coming out of the Ivy closet,
the black closet. then a militant femme,
putting down those men you don't compete with,
compete with all the time, until
their bottoms show & feel like your top.

74

I've heard your poems, your way with words
as if one alphabet were limited, & heard
you play harpsichord to Dick's guitar
& Larry's dulcimer. & no one was straight then,
or gay. there was only sound. & auditors.
you like auditors.

iii.

when you're here, I have to pay attention to you.
know you're waiting for response. needing someone's approval
for the concerts that you missed, the money you didn't have,
the maleness that's not yours. you know more than I know,
you turn our conversation into your listening post.
& I don't trust you.

your needs burst out till anyone nearby
gets filled with shrapnel. I can't help you when you're here.
you'll take my help as you take food or money, then look for
ampler places. I feel you like a nest of crabs & I don't want
to catch the first itch or wait for the spread or powder myself
to get you off. there's nothing I can give will be enough.
there's nothing I can take. sometimes I miss you
--less & less as I feel your hunger, less & less
as I come to care about your needs.

Thoreau House

i.

built as an inn by Highland Light
one parlor one tavern one room
for the innkeeper's family
a small kitchen 3 bedrooms upstairs
now it sits on Old County Road
moved intact from the coast
& being restored by a witch
who owns it & puts overhead
dimming lights in the ceiling.
at twilight unless it rains
or fog comes in over the bay
we see the sun   set.

ii.

five of us live here Peggy Larry & I
& two ghosts one of them dead
only 3 years alcoholic & bitter
but a great lover of tidiness
sometimes she moans & sets red hair on fire
the other is never seen but is
talked about in whispers
whether it be male or female
sometimes we hear it in our dreams
when north wind rattles aluminum siding
& the bobwhite that lives in the bush
wakes at night &   listens.

in the middle of the night

she welcomed us to the street,
good-mouthed us to neighbors,
smiled even when her husband
drank. just two of them lived

there, & one roomer & a frightened
large black dog. Francis Kelley,
retired postal worker, "Kelley,"
she called him. sometimes he

screams in the middle of the night,
shouts to her to bring him something.
his first wife died when he was 50;
her husband drowned when she was 42.

she was a presswoman for the *Globe.*
she told us she "had a heart problem"
& thanked us for shoveling snow
talked about food prices

& the price of heating oil. suddenly
she died in the middle of the night.
the dog barks in the yard now.
Kelley wakes up & drinks.

inside & out
--for S.F.

you're back in Concord
because you get drunk & violent
& your mother called your parole officer
& said you were hitting her

you were in Guantanamo & Viet Nam
where you were ready to die
then you were discharged
but you were there in Boston
when your friend killed a man
felony murder the state calls it
& you went to Walpole

then jail in Buffalo
because you tried to get to Canada
Waltham jail because you saw a swimming pool
on a hot day & took a swim

don't you know you're a white nigger from Southie
whose uncle was gunned down last spring
without swimming rights   &
why can't you learn to crawl?

                    *

when you said you loved me
your wife called to tell me not
to see you   your parole officer
called to ask just what our

relationship was & told me
not to see you   & you know
I don't want to see you   but
sometimes I think about you

moving from a white ghetto
to the army to jail to marriage
to acid to jail again & wonder
what your chances are to find

a real lover   inside or out
before they finally put you away.

failing to disprove that Bette Midler is counter-revolutionary

if every towel is different from a flannel suit
everyone who lives here must be less than naked.

if Kelloggs corn flakes is not necessarily good for corn
if we tried to make our own music & are still failing
only a pot of gold lies under the rainbow.

if every tree whatever nuts & acorns is rooted in mud
the light at the end of the tunnel is still Hoboken.

an hour ago you called & we decided
you'd drive in, we'd eat here I wish
now I'd said I'd thumb in & we could

eat together in town the drive takes
only 15 minutes at the most & it's an
hour later you're still not here I've

picked berries by the Pamet it's
no good of course to think of your ab-
sence all the time you're gone or your

presence when you're here we both
have lives & they are not the same life
but it only takes 15 minutes to drive in

& now it's an hour & I wonder where
you are & what is taking you so long.

starting to subtract

i.

anything. any time. anywhere.
anything--I thought then--was

better than nothing, the rotten
peach better than fasting. & I forgot

who I was in that equation, & I
don't think you ever knew.

ii.

beautiful, I came to call you,
not the outside but what you
kept in, the bait, the seabass
leaping in the surf & diving
down again. but you didn't
always tell the truth or
recognize it, & shifted like
juneberries in july, bright
purple to see but ready to be
spit out.
            I called you *beautiful*
& you began to believe me, but
you found me ugly
for telling you so.

iii.

sensitive, you think of yourself,
& your heart beats daintily.

we must all be careful to give you
depths to drown in, you your own deep sea.

                    iv.
an imagining.
an idiocy.
an ideograph dumb
to the translator's chisel,
an ink spot.
an itch.

                    v.
man.
it's not a word I
use anymore, thinking of myself
or people I have been in love with.
man-
ipulative. male.
making one's own way.
making it alone.
a bouncy raft running the rapids.
you steer better than I'd
ever want to, *man.*

                    vi.
time, you said, I should
give it time. that was your way
--without effort.
& you kept always one
negative step behind me,
speaking your own name.

six ways to train a rhinoceros to jump through an earring

Write a letter to the editor of *National Review*. Forget his name but
address him as "dear sir or madam." Do not expect a free subscription.
Do not want one.

Wade into the Atlantic three miles south of Provincetown.
Wear adhesive tape on your left wrist but do not catch lobsters
until they appear red in the cold water.

Call your grandmother long-distance in Dubuque even though
she runs a laundromat in Fort Lauderdale. Ask her whether cyclones
are fiercer than hurricanes. Hang up before she answers.

Attend the last choir rehearsal before Easter services.
Do a five-minute tap dance on the organ but do not attempt to
become a tenor or a baritone. Or a bass.

Ask the people you know how they have been feeling.
Before they answer give everyone an alka-seltzer wrapped in
purple ribbon. Do not pay for anything.

Think of your life as a set of rubber balls flying through the air
at incredible speeds, one over the other. Think of yourself
as the juggler. Avoid itchy palms.

Remember that in an earlier life you were a rhinoceros trainer.
Remember the broken earrings.

picnicking in Sitka

I wanted to play in the rain but it was hot sun, the
ozone count was high & the humid air was dirtier
than the noxious air I breathed as a boy in Dayton,
not as pure as the air I breathed a decade ago in New York,

& I remember when you used to be able to see stars
at night over the cities. well, it's an old car, Jeb said,
you have to expect it to break down sometimes.
well, the country's two hundred years old, he said,
you can't expect things to last forever.

I wanted to play in the snow but it was summer suddenly
& hot sun for months & months. the icecap began to melt,
& Jeb said, well, you can't expect the icecap to last forever,
besides most bears would rather be brown than white

& wander in forests & swat salmon from the streams.
not even bears like to swim in cold water all the time.

I wanted to play in the rain but the rain never came
& even the snakes were thirsty & flowers on the cacti
grew huge & delicate--red & translucent pink in the
scorching sunlight. I wanted to play in the snow I remember,

but it doesn't snow anymore.

letter to Dick

I want to write you because your stepmother died
& I hadn't known until you wrote that she & you
were closest in age & feelings & chances to talk
with each other & know what you were saying

& because Roberta & you have just had the most horrible
clash of all your clashes & she was not there again
when you needed her & you still see her in every
black car that goes through Ithaca

I want to tell you about the question Tom & I
discussed last night   after I wanted to go to bed
with him the night before & thought he was sleeping
with Rick who wanted to go to bed with me but

he wasn't & I didn't know it & Tom wanted to sleep
with Gary whom he's in love with but who doesn't
love him back the same way: what is the difference
we asked   between love & obsession?

& to tell you that you botched I think the last
stanza of the poem you sent   the life wish death wish
as you so blithely call it--that double motion--
is what I have been living with all year & maybe longer

it comes from living a long time & being scared
& wanting everyone I touch to turn to perfect harmony
& love me back--the same way Williams often botched--
but you can trust him trust you to say

not what is eloquent but what always would be honest
if we only knew   you & I   what we really wanted
& how to love every day every detail of our lives.